Dennis the Menace

"Your Mother's Calling!"

FAWCETT GOLD MEDAL • NEW YORK

"IF YOU RUN OUTA GOLD STARS, WE GOT *LOTS* OF 'EM AT OUR PLACE. MY MOM NEVER USES 'EM."

"THEY'RE NOT GONNA LIVE HERE ALL *YEAR*, MOM! I'LL SEND 'EM OUTSIDE SOON AS SPRING COMES."

"WOULD YOU BELIEVE WE CAN'T FIND *ANYBODY* THAT'S MAKIN' BREAKFAST AT THIS HOUR?"

"IF I NEVER *TRY* NOTHIN'...HOW AM I GONNA FIND OUT WHAT I CAN GET AWAY WITH?"

"DADDY'S LITTLE MAN PUT IN A FULL EIGHT HOURS TODAY."

"HEY! THAT'S PRETTY GOOD! SEE IF YOU CAN HIT THE *PIGGY BANK* WITH THIS NEXT ONE."

"BOY, THAT GINA IS REALLY *SERIOUS* 'BOUT WOMEN'S LIP!"

"QUICK! CALL THE VET...RUFF ATE SOME *CAT FOOD!*"

"WHY ALL THE FUSS? THEY'RE
NOT THAT SCARCE, ARE THEY?"

"AND THEN I SMOTHERED THE CARROTS WITH KETCHUP...
BUT EVEN *THAT* DON'T HELP!"

"THE CLOCK'S LIKE THIS AN' I'M *HUNGRY!*"

"I'M NEVER GOIN' INTO *THAT* KINDA BUSINESS.
I'D GET LONESOME FOR EVERYTHING I SOLD."

"I *DID* WASH 'EM! MAYBE I FOUND A NEW KIND OF DIRT."

"HOW MUCH OLDER DO I HAVE TO GET BEFORE I CAN UNDERSTAND THIS STUFF?"

"IF Mr. WILSON EVER COMES OVER AN' WANTS TO USE OUR BATHROOM...DON'T *LET* HIM !"

"I'M NOT *ALLOWED* TO FIGHT."

"I'M NOT ALLOWED TO DO *LOTS* OF STUFF."

"MY DAD LIKES SUMMER BEST, TOO. HE'S ALREADY GOT MISS JULY ON HIS CALENDAR."

"WHAT A *MESS!* BRING ME SOMETHING TO CLEAN THIS UP!"

"I BETTER PHONE MR. WILSON AN' SEE IF HE'S OKAY! ALL HIS DOORS AN' WINDOWS ARE *LOCKED*...AN' HIS DOORBELL DON'T WORK!"

"BE NICE TO THIS KID. HE GAVE ME A NICKEL TO INNERDUCE HIM."

"HEY! NOT THAT NICE!"

"DID YOU HEAR *THAT*? MARGARET SAYS SHE'S BUILDING A *SNOW PERSON!*"

"THE SNOW SHOVEL ... LESSEE .... I WAS USIN' IT
FOR SOMETHING JUS' THIS SUMMER ..."

"HOLD THE SOUP...HE FELL DOWN AGAIN!"

"ONE SNOWSHOE ISN'T MUCH GOOD... WHO ELSE DO WE KNOW THAT PLAYS TENNIS?"

"CHEER UP, MR. WILSON! PRETTY SOON YOU'LL BE CUTTIN' GRASS AND PULLIN' WEEDS AGAIN."

"HEY, DID YOU KNOW MR. WILSON HAS A *BRASS MONKEY*?"

"I SAID... ANOTHER NICE THING ABOUT A BLIZZARD...YOU CAN'T EVEN HEAR YOUR MOTHER CALLING YOU!"

"WILL YOU MAKE ME A *SNOWMAN*
BEFORE YOU GO TO WORK?"

"LET'S GET A *SNOWMOBILE*, DAD! WE COULD TRADE-IN THE LAWNMOWER AN' THE HOSE AN' GARDEN TOOLS..THE LAWN CHAIRS, THE WADING POOL AN'..."

"ARE WE REALLY GONNA MOVE TO FLORIDA TONIGHT?"

"I GOTTA HANG UP NOW, GINA, BECAUSE MY MOM AN'
DAD ARE GONNA TRY TO GIVE ME NOSE DROPS."

"I'LL TELL YA WHY I NEED FIVE SAMWICHES...I GOT FOUR CUSTOMERS WAITIN' *OUTSIDE!*"

"WELL...YA LEARN SOMETHIN' EVERY DAY."

"DID YOU PEOPLE KNOW YA CAN'T MAKE PANCAKES IN A TOASTER?"

"MOM SAYS NEVER *MIND* WHAT'S FOR DINNER ...
TAKE YOUR CHANCES WITH THE REST OF US."

"I'M JUST LOOKIN' FOR THE RING IN YOUR NOSE."

"PLEASE PASS THE CARROTS."

"HA HA·HEE HEE·HO HO·HAHA!"

"YOU SHOULDA ASKED ME ABOUT TANTRUMS, JOEY.
RULE ONE: DON'T BANG YOUR HEAD ON THE FLOOR..."

"HEY! YOU LOOKIN' FOR DIRT OR **GOLD**?"

"IF MR. WILSON TRYS TO CALL YA, REMEMBER...
HE'S *ALWAYS* GROUCHY."

"STOP WORRYING, DEWEY! BY TOMORROW MORNING
IT'LL ALL BE COVERED OVER WITH SNOW."

"GEE! YA KNOW IT'S A WHOLE DIFFERENT WORLD UP HERE!"

"HI, MR. WILSON...HOW'S MY COLD?"

"WHAT DO YA MEAN HE'S JUST LIKE ONE OF THE FAMILY? HE *IS* ONE OF THE FAMILY!"

"WHEN I SIT THEM, I SIT THEM, MRS. MITCHELL."

"NO KIDDIN'...SHE REALLY *SAT* ON ME!"

"IT'S A GUEST TOWEL, ISN'T IT?
I'M A GUEST, AREN'T I?"

"SHE WAS ON THE AIR ALL MORNING, MRS. HACKER, BUT SHE'LL BE BROADCASTING AGAIN SOON AS WE HAVE OUR LUNCH."

"YES, I REALIZE IT'S FOUR O'CLOCK IN THE MORNING, HENRY...BUT WE'VE HAD A *BURGLAR* SCARE..."

"...AND THOUGHT YOU MIGHT WANT TO LOOK AROUND AND SEE IF ANYTHING IS *MISSING*."

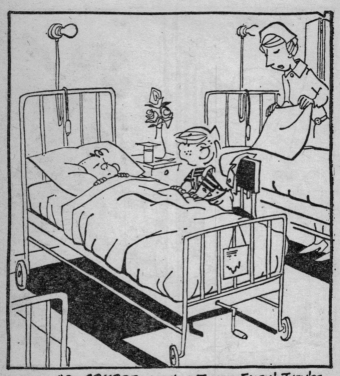

"OF *COURSE* THERE'S A TONSIL FAIRY! THEY'RE JUST NOT TELLIN' YA ABOUT HIM!"

"BOY! WOULD WE EVER BE A *HAPPY FAMILY* IF WE ATE HERE ALL THE TIME!"

"WHEN YOU GET DONE WITH YOUR FACE, ARE YA GONNA TRY TO FIX *DAD'S* ?"

"MY LITTLE TRUCK IS OKAY, MR. WILSON...
ARE *YOU* ALL RIGHT?"

"DON'T WASTE TIME SAYIN' NICE THINGS TO THE BABY...HE WON'T KNOW WHAT YOU'RE TALKIN' ABOUT ANYWAY."

"STICK AROUND. I'LL BE BACK SOON
AS I HAVE MY BATH."

"HE'S NOT BENT OUT OF SHAPE...
HE *ALWAYS* LOOKS LIKE THAT."

"I THOUGHT I WAS IMAGINING IT, BUT HE ACTUALLY *DOES* GET THEM DIRTY FASTER THAN I CAN WASH THEM!"

"GOT ANY PETS YOU'D LIKE SOMEBODY TO TAKE FOR A WALK?"

"LOOK AT WHAT YOUR *NIGHTGOWN* IS DOIN'!"

"YOU'D BE WEAK, TOO, IF ALL YA GOT TO EAT
WAS CHICKEN FLAVOR *HOT WATER!*"

"IT WAS ALL YOUR FAULT!"

"PARTLY YOUR FAULT?"

"DENNIS CAN'T COME OUT JUST NOW, JOEY."

"YEAH...I'M *BUSY!*"

"HE DIDN'T *REALLY* KISS HER...THEY GOT STUNT MEN FOR THAT KINDA STUFF."

"NEXT TIME I'LL TAKE CARE OF *HIM* AND YOU HANDLE HIS DUMB *DOG!*"

"I'M SO HUNGRY I COULD EAT A *CARROT!*"

"EH...THAT'S JUST A *FINGER* OF *SPEECH*, Y'KNOW."

"I DON'T WANTA BUY NOTHIN'...I JUST WANTA *FEEL* SOME OF THE STUFF I CAN'T TOUCH AT HOME."

"ANOTHER HONEST THING ABOUT MR. WILSON...HE NEVER PERTENDS HE'S GLAD TO *SEE* YA."

"THERE ARE *SEVERAL* REASONS WHY THE BUTLER COULDN'T HAVE DONE IT."

"I FELL IN THE MUD... THEY JUST CAME
ALONG TO HEAR YOU SCREECH."

"BUT THE POLICEMAN WAS REAL NICE. HE EVEN LET DAD BLOW UP A BALLOON!"

"THAT'S NOT VERY FUNNY."

"YOU SAID IT WOULD BE *FUNNY*."

"IS THAT SOMEONE AT THE FRONT DOOR?"

"NAW...IT'S JUST OL' RUFF DOIN' HIS *THING!*"

"MARGARET SAYS THEY GOT TERR'TORIES THEY FIGHT FOR AN' PERTECT...JUST LIKE MR. WILSON."

"I'M ONLY GONNA STAY OUT A FEW MINUTES... I JUST WANTA FEEL SOME APRIL SPLASHIN' ON ME."

"*ALL* HOSPITALS HAVE VISITING HOURS, JOEY! WE'LL JUST TELL 'EM WE'RE *RELATIVES*."

"MY FOLKS KEEP TALKIN' ABOUT *MOVIN'* SOMEWHERES."

"IS IT WRONG TO MAKE SOMEONE *HAPPY*?"

"WELL..THERE GOES HALF OF MR. WILSON'S NEW GARDEN."

"HOW COME PEOPLE ALWAYS HAVE TO GO TO THE HOSPITAL FOR BABIES? DON'T THEY EVER DELIVER?"

"OKAY, JOEY...PUT IN YOUR PENNY AN' WE'LL GET OFF ONE AT A TIME SO MARGARET CAN FIGGER OUT HOW MUCH WE WEIGH."

"MOM WANTS TO KNOW WHAT YOU THINK YOU'RE *DOIN'* DOWN HERE."

"BOYS DON'T WRESTLE
WITH GIRLS!"

"DID YA HEAR *THAT*, GINA?
GET *OFFA* ME!"

"I HOPE YA FIND HER."

"JUST SOME LADY LOOKIN' FOR THE MOTHER OF A TERRIBLE LITTLE KID."

"OKAY, DENNIS...YOU'RE THE BOSS."

"WATCH OUT FOR THAT ONE IN ABOUT TEN YEARS."

" SHHH... LISTEN... THERE HE GOES AGAIN... DENNIS IS TRYING TO IMITATE A *DUCK*!"

"WHY DON'T YOU TRY THE WILSONS...WE'RE NOT OPEN TODAY."

"YOU BETTER GET IN HERE WITH ME AN' RUFF...
I'LL EXPLAIN LATER."

"HOW DO YA TELL TIME, DENNIS?"

"STICK YOUR HEAD IN HERE AN' *YELL*, I GUESS."

"WHAT ARE WE RAISIN' *THIS* YEAR, MR. WILSON?"

"*A*WWWWWWWW!"

"*HERE'S* ONE! I THOUGHT YOU SAID THE PRICES IN
THIS STORE WERE OUTA SIGHT!"

"I THINK I'LL GO BACK TO TAKIN' *NAPS* IN THE AFTERNOON."

"IS ANYBODY AWAKE ENOUGH TO LOOK UP THE NUMBER OF THE MAN THAT CLEANS CARPETS?"

"HI, MR. WILSON! YOU AN' YOUR GARDEN
GONNA TRY IT AGAIN THIS YEAR?"

"HE IS *NOT* LAZY...HE'S JUST SAVIN' HIMSELF IN CASE SOMETHIN' *IMPORTANT* COMES UP."

"I COULD *TELL* HIM TO ROLL OVER AN' HE'D *DO* IT...
BUT WE'D BOTH THINK IT WAS PRETTY SILLY."

"LET ME SEE YOUR *HANDS.*"

"FOR A MINUTE THERE, I THOUGHT SHE WAS GONNA *FAINT.*"

"LET ME TELL YOU WHAT *YOUR* SON DID TODAY!"

"YOU MEAN MY POOR, MOTHERLESS SON?"

"HE'S RIGHT, YOU KNOW. NOT *EVERY* KID IN THIS NEIGHBORHOOD COULD 'BUST A CROWBAR'."

"WHEW! AS THEY SAY, MRS. MITCHELL... ALL SYSTEMS ARE **GO** FOR ANOTHER SIX MONTHS."

"THIS IS A *SWELL* KIND OF BIRTHDAY PARTY! I WISH MORE OF OUR MOTHERS WOULD GET FED UP!"

"YOU'LL LIKE IT HERE...IT'S A REAL FRIENDLY NEIGHBORHOOD."

"YA WANNA FIGHT?"

"OH, *GOOD!* YOU FOUND MY CHAIN AN' PADLOCK!"

"OH-OH! HERE COMES ANOTHER SOAP COMMERCIAL."

"IT'S SPRIG, ALL RIGHT...MR. WILSON IS TALKID' TO HIS TULIBS, BARGARET'S TALKID' TO BIRDS AND BY DOSE IS RUDDID'."

'Awww, Mom...it's *SPRING!* I don't need walkin' shoes...I need *RUNNIN'* shoes!'

"THAT 'FUNNY SMELL' MEANS YOU SHOULD STAY *OFF* MR. WILSON'S LAWN TODAY."

"WHAT CAN YA DO WHEN
THERE'S NOTHIN' TO *DO*?"

"*LIVE* A LITTLE!"

"MOM...IS THERE SOME WAY WE CAN FLUSH THE *WHOLE BATHROOM*?"

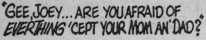
"GEE, JOEY... ARE YOU AFRAID OF *EVERTHING* 'CEPT YOUR MOM AN' DAD?"

"I'M 'FRAID OF MY DADDY, TOO."

"WELL, THAT'S *ANOTHER* THING I
CAN'T GET AWAY WITH NO MORE."

"IT PROBABLY SAYS NOT TO DO SOMETHIN',
BUT I DON'T KNOW WHAT."

"SPEAK UP, HONEY... I CAN HARDLY HEAR YOU."

"I'LL TALK TO YA LATER... THERE'S SOMEBODY ELSE ON THIS LINE."

"BRING ALL THE PAPER TOWELS YA CAN FIND, JOEY! I'M TOO BUSY TO ANSWER A LOTTA QUESTIONS RIGHT NOW!"

"OKAY...THE *FIRST* TIME YA DO SOMETHIN', IT'S **CUTE**. BUT YA GOTTA KEEP COMIN' UP WITH NEW STUFF ALL THE TIME."

"WELL, WE FOUND THE WRENCH..."

"NOW WE GOTTA FIND SOME-THIN' TO *USE* IT ON."

"DON'T TRY TO LEARN ME NOTHIN' TODAY, MARGARET. MY BRAINS ARE TAKIN' A VACATION."

"I'M SORRY ABOUT YOUR COAT, MISTER. I NEVER HAD A KETCHUP BOTTLE DO *THAT* BEFORE!"

"I S'POSE I WAS HOME WITH THE SITTER WHILE ALL THIS WAS GOIN' ON."

"I'M NEVER SURE WHERE I STAND WITH YOU, MR. WILSON."

"OVER THERE WILL DO."

"YA CAN'T PLAY *ANYWHERE* IN THIS NEIGHBORHOOD! WHEN I GET BIG, THE FIRST THING I'M GONNA BUY IS A *EMPTY LOT!*"

"I TELL YA THAT'S *HIM!* HE'S WEARIN' PLAIN CLOTHES SO HE CAN *CHECK-UP* ON US!"

"DON'T LET *THAT* FOOL YA ... HE LIKES TO SEE ME ALL DRESSED UP 'CAUSE IT MEANS I'M *GOIN'* SOMEWHERES."

"HOW 'BOUT GETTIN' ME A JOB AT YOUR PLACE, DAD? I DON'T GET ALONG VERY GOOD WITH ALL THESE *RETIRED* PEOPLE."

"WAIT, I'LL GO *WITH* YA! YOU SHOULDN'T BE WALKING AROUND ALONE WITH A WHOLE DOLLAR."

"YOUR MOTHER SAYS HER CHOCOLATE CAKE IS DONE."

"SO, SEND HIM HOME IF HE WANTS A PIECE."

"WHERE ARE YOU PEOPLE GONNA MOVE TO WHEN I GET MARRIED AN' HAVE A FAMILY OF MY OWN?"